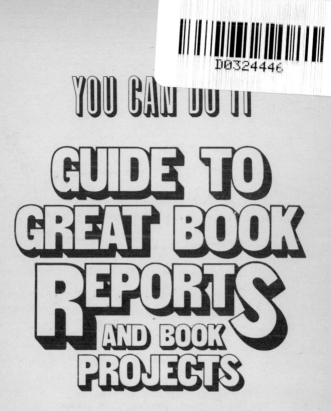

YOU CAN DO IT

GUIDE TO GREAT BOOK REPORTS AND BOOK PROJECTS

by Leslie Lauderdale
illustrated by Ed Francis

To my writing friends,
Bernice Torregrossa and Connie Walley.

Published by Worthington Press, Inc.
7099 Huntley Road, Worthington, Ohio 43085

Copyright © 1989 by Worthington Press, Inc.

Published in the United States of America

10 9 8 7 6 5 4 3 2

ISBN 0-87406-379-5

The author gratefully acknowledges the assistance given by Wendy Ramsey, Children's Librarian at the Dublin (Ohio) Branch of the Public Library of Columbus and Franklin County.

CONTENTS

1 Busy Work or Basic Work?

Book reports have been around just about as long as people have been telling stories. Imagine one caveperson saying to another, "I just read this great cave wall about mastodon hunting. You really should read it, Zog." Or an ancient Egyptian saying to a friend, "Here, take this papyrus roll. It's all about the latest rock stars. You'll love it!" These may not

7

sound like book reports to you, but a book report is just a way for people to share their feelings about a book they have read. When someone says, "I read a really good book about...," and continues with either some details about the story and characters or an opinion of the book, you have the beginning of a book report.

There are several ways to do book reports. Your teacher may have specific guidelines that he wants you to follow for a *written report*. Another teacher might require a *book project*, such as a poster or a skit, that relates to a part of the story. Some teachers may even ask that you give an *oral report*.

If you have been assigned a written or oral report, you'll need to read Chapters 1 through 4. Chapter 5 contains special information on doing book projects. For these types of special projects you should read everything except Chapter 4.

Four Basics of Book Reports

Written reports, oral reports, and book projects are all book reports, but they differ from one another in form. We'll discuss each of these types of reports and how they're all different from one another later in this book. Right now, let's look at the basic building blocks that they all share. Each kind of book report should do the following four things.

1 Retell the story

The most basic step in doing any project is building a good foundation. The foundation for your book report is made up of the details that you use to retell the story. Retelling the story means that you describe the actions or events that were important to the outcome of the book. This is the frame you will use for the remainder of your report.

9

2 Describe the characters

An author creates each character for a reason. Your book report should give details about the main characters, and it should tell why they are important to the story. A book report that doesn't describe the characters is like chocolate-chip cookies without the chocolate chips. They might taste okay, but there's definitely something missing!

3 Express your opinion

When you read a book, you form an immediate opinion. You either like it or dislike it. Maybe your feelings are even stronger. Did you think that it was the

worst book ever written? Did you love it so much that you were sorry it was over when you finished it? Maybe you loved the characters. Or, maybe you hated their guts. You might have thought the book was boring, funny, thrilling, scary, or a total waste of time.

The reasons why you liked or disliked the book are crucial to your book report. What made you feel this way? Your book report is not complete without giving your opinion and then supporting it with reasons and information.

4 Explore the author's meaning

This fourth building block may not seem very important at first. However, you might have to think a little bit before answering the question, "Just what was the author trying to say in this book?"

The author may not be trying to make some big, important statement. A good answer might be something simple but accurate. "The author was saying that having an older brother can be both a pleasure and a pain" might be a suitable answer. Some books might have a more obvious moral, or deeper meaning. "The author was saying that if you work hard, you can overcome any problem" would be a better reply in that case. Some books try to teach you about what's right and what's wrong. Some books just want to make you laugh, cry, or get chills of terror up and down your spine.

A Few Good Reasons Why

Why would your teacher want you to do a book report? She probably had a couple of goals in mind when she gave the assignment. Book reports will help you become a better student in many ways. Here are a few examples of how writing a

book report will help you to become a better student. Writing a book report accomplishes the following tasks.

• Proves that you read the book

Okay, it's true. Sometimes you have to *prove* to your teacher that you have done your assigned reading. More importantly, a book report will reveal whether or not you actually understood the story that the author was telling.

• Shares your book with others

The best part about reading a good book is being able to share the story with your friends. When a friend tells you about a really neat book that he's read, doesn't it make you want to head straight to the library or bookstore and pick up a

copy for yourself?

When your classmates discuss the books that they've read, you get information that will help you to decide which fabulous books you'll want to read for your own enjoyment—and which dogs you'll want to avoid at all cost!

• **Makes you think about your reading**

If you know when you start reading a book that you will have to write a report, you may read it more carefully. As you read, you may think about the author's reasons for writing the story or about a character's reasons for doing something. Thinking while you are reading will give you some direction, and it will help you to organize your report.

- **Helps you express your opinion**

Your opinion is important. Learning how to express your opinion effectively is a valuable lesson.

Have you ever been frustrated when someone says that something is true "just because" or "because I say so"? "Because"

isn't a reason. It's what you say before you give your reason. Saying something without supporting it with a reason isn't sound thinking, and it will frustrate anyone who reads your book report.

Giving your opinion about a book and then backing it up with evidence from the book will give your report greater impact. The ability to influence and persuade other people through your writing is a skill that will be important for the rest of your life. Almost any job you'll have will involve some writing, or what's known as "communication skills." And these skills are getting more important every day!

• **Prepares you for the "real world"**

All of the skills that you use to write a book report can be used to write other types of reports. Annual reports, progress reports, monthly reports, or weekly reports are a way of life for many business people and community volunteers.

Being able to organize and condense information is important in writing book reports, and this ability will be important to you later when you're an adult.

Reports in the "Real World"

Written reports aren't always about books, but all of them *do* use the same basic skills. Some of the ways you might use the skills that you learn in writing book reports are as follows:

- writing a sales report for a candy sale that's put on by a youth group

- writing a progress report on a Scout camping trip

- writing a membership report on a school group

2 First, You Read the Book

The first step in writing a great book report is to pick up a book and start reading! Sometimes that sounds easier than it really is. Strange things can happen between the time you get the assignment and the time you write the report.

Raiding the library on a book-finding mission sounds simple enough, but there are all kinds of dangers lurking right around the corner. You could choose a boring book or the wrong book. You might even put off starting to read the book until you're forced to read all night in order to finish in time.

First Things First

There are a few easy ways to avoid these and other problems. Your first step is to make sure your teacher will accept the book that you've chosen before you start reading. Ask the following questions:

- **Is there an assigned booklist?**

Your teacher may assign a specific book title or ask that you choose one from a particular list. Your teacher has carefully chosen the books on the list. If your teacher has a list, make sure that your book is on it. If you aren't sure if there is an approved list, find out!

- **Do you need your teacher's approval?**

Even if your teacher doesn't have a booklist, you might have to have your book approved before you start reading it. Make sure that you don't get going in the wrong direction by choosing a book that doesn't meet with your teacher's approval.

✓ Don't Live With Your Mistakes!

If there isn't any particular booklist for you to choose from, then you're on your own. How can you make sure the book you choose isn't so boring that it would put you, your guinea pig, and your next-door neighbor to sleep? How do you choose a book that's so exciting it will keep you awake all night?

Well, picking out a book for a report isn't an exact science. You can expect to make a few mistakes along the way. Sometimes a really great cover will mislead you into believing that what is inside the book is just as great. You know the old saying, "You can't judge a book by its cover!"

Sometimes the title of the book may sound interesting, or the book's cover or jacket may appeal to you. These are all good reasons for picking up the book to begin with, but don't let them be your only guides.

Rule 1

If the book isn't worth reading, then don't bother reading it!

The first rule of writing a report is not to finish a book that is boring, silly, or just plain bad. Don't waste your time reading a book that you don't enjoy, when there are millions of entertaining books just waiting for you out there.

Rule 2

Read what you are assigned to read.

Of course, if you were assigned a specific book for your report, you have to follow the second rule of report writing.

Your teacher has read lots of books. He probably took courses in college to learn all about the best books. Any book on your teacher's list is going to be a good one. Whichever one you choose, give it a chance. Don't give up on the book after reading only the first three pages!

What's the Problem Here?

Before you discard a book as being a big bore, think about what it was that you didn't like about it. If you can figure out *why* you didn't like it, chances are you won't make that mistake a second time. The following are just a few things to look for.

- **You have difficulty understanding the book.**

Was the book too hard to read? Did it use words that you didn't understand or language that seemed old-fashioned? A book that is written for an older person or for someone with a larger vocabulary than yourself will seem boring to you because you don't fully understand the story.

Some books that were written a long time ago use words and phrases that sound weird to us because they aren't common in today's speech. If you can't understand what's happening, you just won't appreciate the book.

- **The reading level is too young.**

Was the book too easy to read? Did it seem to be written for a much younger person than yourself? If you have outgrown a particular author or type of book, it can seem childish and boring to you. Don't select a book just because you think it will be easy to read. If you aren't able to get involved with a story, you won't be able to write a good book report about it.

TOO YOUNG

TOO HARD

TOO LONG

• **The book is too long.**

Don't make the mistake of choosing a book that's too long. You have a limited time to do your reading. Save that 600-page novel for summertime or Christmas vacation. It can be pretty discouraging to pick up a book that weighs as much as your little brother when your report is due in three days!

Four Quick Cures for the Blah Book Blues

Suppose someone gave you a free pass to Disney World, and you could go on all the rides for free! Which one would you choose first? What if someone handed you the key to the world's biggest bakery, and told you to dig in. What would you eat first? Doughnuts? Eclairs? Chocolate-chip cookies?

Well, sometimes having all the books in the library to choose from can be a little overwhelming, too. If your teacher says that you can read whatever you want for your book report, you might need a little guidance. Since you don't want to get stuck with a blah book, try the following four pointers.

1 Read something by your favorite author.

It's great to read a new book by an author whose stories you have enjoyed before. You can always depend on some authors to turn out interesting and entertaining books. If you have a favorite writer whose tales always keep you happily reading until the end, grab her latest book, and get going!

Kids' Favorite Authors

Judie Angell	Mollie Hunter
John Bellairs	E.L. Konigsburg
Judy Blume	Madeleine L'Engle
Betsy Byars	Lois Lowry
Beverly Cleary	Scott O'Dell
Ellen Conford	Lurlene McDaniel
Jamie Gilson	Katherine Paterson
James Howe	Janet Adele Bloss
Irene Hunt	Alida E. Young

2 **Read something interesting.**

This sounds a little silly. You wouldn't want to read about something that is *uninteresting*, right? When you are selecting a book, think about picking out one that is a little different from your usual selections.

If you've never read science fiction, check out a book like the *Foundling and Other Tales of Prydain* by Lloyd Alexander. If you like love stories, you don't have to limit yourself to teenage romances. Try something by Jane Austen or Charlotte Bronte.

Science Fiction Sampler of Tales by Lloyd Alexander

Foundling and Other Tales of Prydain
The Book of Three
The Black Cauldron
The Castle of Llyr
Taran Wanderer
The High King

3 Read something "tried and true."

Some books have been around so long that your grandparents could have read them. These classic tales have survived over the years for a good reason—they're great books that tell an interesting story in an exciting way.

You may want to select one of these books for a change of pace. It might impress your teacher, and you'll learn a lot about the world of literature.

Classics

Little Women, Louisa May Alcott
Sounder, William Armstrong
Caddie Woodlawn, Carol R. Brink
"Henry Huggins" series, Beverly Cleary
"Ramona" series, Beverly Cleary
The Black Stallion, Walter Farley
Johnny Tremain, Esther Forbes
A Wrinkle in Time, Madeleine L'Engle
The Chronicles of Narnia, C.S. Lewis
Story of Doctor Dolittle, Hugh Lofting

Homer Price, Robert McCloskey
Anne of Green Gables, L.M. Montgomery
Where the Red Fern Grows, Wilson Rawls
"Henry Reed" series, Keith Robertson
The Witch of Blackbird Pond,
   Elizabeth G. Speare
Little House on the Prairie,
   Laura Ingalls Wilder

---

4 **Read something your friends liked.**

Your friends may be the best source of information on books. Ask around to see which books they have enjoyed. Ask them why they liked a particular book. When they recommend a book, they're giving you a miniature book report. You will be giving the same information back to your teacher (in a more polished form, of course!) when you sit down and write your book report.

Kids Pick Their Favorite Books

Joan Aiken	*Wolves of Willoughby Chase*
Lynne R. Banks	*The Indian in the Cupboard*
	Return of the Indian
Bertrand Brinley	*Mad Scientists' Club*
Sheila Burnford	*The Incredible Journey*
Oliver Butterworth	*The Enormous Egg*
Roald Dahl	*The BFG, Boy, The Witches*
Edward Eager	*Half Magic*
John D. Fitzgerald	*"Great Brain" series*
Louise Fitzhugh	*Harriet the Spy*
Jean C. George	*Julie of the Wolves*
Fred Gipson	*Old Yeller*
Beatrice Gormley	*Mail Order Wings*
E.A. Haas	*Incognito Mosquito*
	"Private Insective" series
Mary D. Hahn	*Daphne's Book*
	Wait 'Till Helen Comes
E.L. Konigsburg	*From the Mixed-up Files of Mrs. Basil E. Frankweiler*
Lois Lowry	*Rabble Starkey*
	"Anastasia" series
Lurlene McDaniel	*Six Months to Live*
Michael J. Pellowski	*Double Trouble*
Robert C. O'Brien	*Mrs. Frisby and the Rats of Nimh*
Ellen Raskin	*The Westing Game*
Willo D. Roberts	*The View from the Cherry Tree*
Mary Rodgers	*A Billion for Boris*
Sarah Sargent	*Watermusic*
Janet Adele Bloss	*30 Ways to Dump a Sister*
	My Brother the Creep
William Steig	*Abel's Island*
Alida E. Young	*What's Wrong with Daddy?*
	Megan the Klutz

Your teacher will warn you. Your mother will beg you. Your father will nag you. Still you might be tempted to put off reading your book until the last possible moment. Even if you've taken a speed-reading course, you could find yourself with too many pages and too little time.

After you've chosen a book, you still have to open it up and read it. A simple way to spread out the amount of reading you need to do in the available time is to follow the Pages vs. Time Formula.

Let's say that you have a 100-page book and 10 days until your report is due. First, subtract a few days to allow yourself enough time to write your report. Let's be generous and allow 5 days for writing the report. Now you have 5 days left to read a 100-page book. (There are 10 days until your report is due, minus 5 days to write the report. That leaves 5 days for you to read the book.) Divide 5 into 100 to see how many pages you must read each day to finish your book on time. Reading 20 pages a day is easy, but trying to read 100 pages in a day isn't quite as easy! Pace yourself. Allow yourself time to enjoy your book. Give yourself time to think about what you are reading before you start writing. Don't put off getting started so long that you have to do it all in a mad rush. Reading should be fun!

It's definitely not fun if you're so pressed for time that you have to read while you're brushing your teeth (besides, how are you going to get toothpaste off your book?).

How to Read a Book

Reading a book isn't anything new to you, of course. But when you read a book for a report, you should pay careful attention to a few things.

• Read the entire book.

The first rule is to start reading the book, and then finish it! Don't try to cheat. Don't skim the pages. Don't guess at the ending. Don't check out the video. Don't just read the back of the book jacket. Read the whole book—every page of it!

There are no shortcuts when you read for your report. Do you really think your teacher can't tell the difference between a book report that was loosely based on a

Saturday morning cartoon and one that was written on a book that you actually read and thought about? Come on, teachers are smarter than that!

• **Read when you are alert.**
Don't start reading your book when you're tired and ready for a long nap. Start when you are alert, and your mind and body are awake. Get comfortable—but not too comfortable. Kick off your shoes. But don't curl up in bed, or you might find yourself in the middle of a dream, instead of in the middle of a book.

You should also make sure that you have the proper amount of light to read. Reading in poor light strains your eyes

and can give you headaches. It's kind of hard to enjoy a book when you can't see the pages.

- **Read actively.**

If your teacher tells you to "read actively," she doesn't mean to do jumping jacks between chapters! To read actively means to keep your mind, and even your body, actively involved in the reading process.

If you own the book and it's okay to write in it, you could underline important parts of the story or write in the margins of the page. Sometimes it helps you to keep track of the setting or characters if you mark the pages where they are introduced.

Of course, you should *never* write in a book that you don't own, such as a library book or a schoolbook. Instead, take notes on a piece of paper as you're reading.

There are some work sheets in Chapter 3 that will help you keep track of information for your book report. Keep them handy while you are reading, and fill out the important information as you come across it. These will be very useful to you later when you actually start to write your book report.

Choosing a good book, having your teacher approve it, starting to read it, and then finishing it will get you started on the road to a great book report. You can do it!

3 Literary Lingo

There are some new words that you'll discover when you start writing about books. "Literary lingo," the words used to describe parts of stories, may seem a little complicated at first. But don't worry. You'll get the hang of these new words pretty quickly. If you had just started to ride a bike and you had never heard words like *wheelie, BMX,* or *freestyling,* you'd catch on soon enough. It's the same sort of thing when you first start writing about books.

Even when your teacher assigned your book report, he may have used a few words that you weren't familiar with. Words like *plot, major and minor characters*, and *climax* are important when you are learning about books and writing your book report.

In this chapter, we'll take a close look at some of this literary lingo.

APPLES   AND   ORANGES

Comparing Apples to Oranges

You don't eat all kinds of fruit the same way. You don't have to peel an apple before taking a bite, but you'd probably want to peel a banana before eating it. Books are different from each other, too. And different books require different kinds of reports. Before you start writing your report, know what kind of book you've chosen. Trying to do the same kind of report on different types of books is like gulping down all kinds of fruit with the peel on. It's okay for some books, but it's not going to work for others.

There are two general kinds of books.

1 Fiction

Fiction is writing that is based on something the author has imagined. Some examples of fiction are fantasy, science fiction, mystery, romance, and westerns.

2 Nonfiction

Nonfiction books are based on factual information or on a true story. They are not made up. The subject matter is researched and studied before the author writes the book. Autobiographies, books written by a person about herself; biographies, books written about a person by someone else; histories; and how-to guides, such as this book, are examples of nonfiction books.

✓ Great Expectations

Fiction and nonfiction are different types of writing. It would be difficult to write the same kind of book report about a fiction book and a nonfiction book because the elements, the ingredients that make up the book, are different. Remember the banana and the apple?

Our expectations of a book are often

based on the familiar elements that make up that type of book. If you read a mystery and you figured out "who done it" in the very first chapter, you'd be disappointed because the book didn't mystify you as you expected it to. On the other hand, if you read a nonfiction book about the Civil War, you'd be confused if it tried to make a mystery out of who won the war. Everybody knows who won the war. Its job as a historical book is to tell you all about an actual event.

The people, places, and action in a story are the ingredients that keep you turning the pages until the end. The way these elements are presented in a book are important because they help the book do its job successfully. The four common elements of books are: characters, setting, plot, and mood.

Let's look at each one to see how it supports the story and helps the book to be a success.

Characters

A book's characters are the people (or animals) that bring it to life. They make things happen. Often an interesting character will keep you reading a story just to see how he manages to get out of a predicament.

The author makes a special effort to create characters you can care for. Vivid,

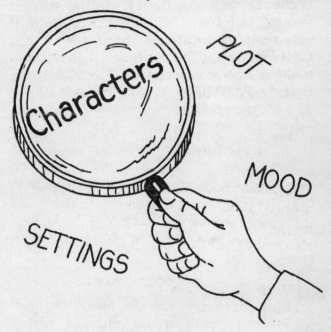

colorful descriptions along with dialogue reveal what kinds of people the characters are. The author's ability to make characters seem "real" is one of the most important ingredients in a successful book.

NON-FICTION
Abraham Lincoln

FICTION

The characters in a nonfiction book such as an autobiography or biography serve the same purpose as the characters in a fiction book. The biggest difference is that the people are real in nonfiction, and they are imaginary in fiction.

There are two kinds of characters in a story.

1 Main characters

Main characters are the ones who play an essential role in the outcome of the story. The book is centered on them and the problems that they encounter. They are a part of the action most of the time.

There can be several main characters in a book. If one character is more important than any other, she is called a protagonist, or focus character. The villain, or bad guy, is called the antagonist. This character causes problems for the protagonist.

Main characters are set apart from less important characters by the changes that take place in their lives. As the story unfolds, each main character will change or grow in some way. These changes might be very important, such as when a character learns to live with a disability or survives being stranded on a desert island. Or, the changes might be unimportant, such as when a character quits biting her fingernails or learns to fly a kite.

2 Minor characters

Minor characters are all the "little people" who come and go throughout the story. These people are not important to the outcome of the book. They don't really grow or change. We don't get to know them very well because the author has created them to perform a certain job, such as deliver the mail or drive the school bus, and then move on. But, in a

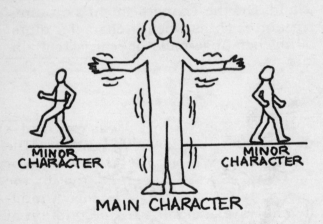

MINOR CHARACTER

MINOR CHARACTER

MAIN CHARACTER

good book, even the minor characters are interesting and seem real to us. We care about them, too. We just don't know as much about them.

Testing for Character

If you are not sure whether a character is a main character or a minor character, try the following test.

1. Is the character essential to the outcome of the story?
2. Does the character grow or change during the story?
3. Is the character present in most scenes of the story?

Main characters will do one or all of these things.

Mood

The feelings you get when you read a book don't happen by accident. The author has created the atmosphere, or mood, to play an important role in the story. An author creates the mood in different ways, including the description of the characters, the setting, and the dialogue. The mood involves us and our emotions in the story. The mood can be almost any emotion that you feel. Can you think of a book you've read that has a happy mood, a sad mood, or a scary mood?

✓ Setting

The setting is almost as important to a story as its characters. The setting is where and when a story takes place. The way the author presents this information helps to create a vivid picture in our minds. Think of the setting of your favorite book. How does the author create and describe it?

Just as you were able to "see" the characters in the story, you should be able to picture the place and time that the story occurs. The setting performs three jobs.

1 It defines a time period.

The time period that the author chooses has an important effect on the book. Time periods can be anything from an era (the Civil War era, prehistoric times, or even the future) to a season.

If the author has placed the story in the past, you can be sure that the setting is crucial to the story. The life-styles of the people and the way that they dressed and talked were very different from the way they are today. These things will affect the action and the characters of the book. For instance, a book that is set in ancient

Rome would not be about a boy who wanted a new pair of basketball shoes or a BMX bicycle!

Even if the author has set the story in modern times, pay close attention to the time of year. Different seasons mean different activities for the characters.

2 It describes a place.

The place where the story occurs is also an important part of the setting. Your story may take place in a small town, in a foreign country, on board a ship, or even in outer space! Each of these different settings will influence what the story is about and what happens to the characters.

3 **It creates a mood.**

Often the setting is central to the mood that is created in the book. A creepy forest, a dark castle, or a haunted mansion could really add an important ingredient to the story.

The setting can create an atmosphere of suspense, happiness, dread, or anything at all. Think of the setting of a book that you've read recently. What was the mood created by the setting? How did the author create this mood?

If a house is bright and cheerful, it would be difficult to imagine it as being haunted. A lonely farmhouse in the middle of a huge prairie says a lot about what sort of people live there and what kinds of things will happen in the story.

Plot

The plot of a story is the action that takes place and moves the story to its conclusion. The plot presents the main

characters with challenges that make them grow or change.

A story's plot follows an established pattern. The five parts of this pattern are the initial complication, the rising action, the climax, the anticlimax, and the resolution. Let's take a closer look at each one of these elements.

• **Initial complication**

When the story begins, the characters are enjoying the calm before the storm.

That's because the author's first task is to present the characters, the setting, and the mood of the book through description and dialogue.

Once you have learned a little bit about the characters, the author presents more and more details of their current situations. The first significant incident or action that creates a challenge for the main character or characters is the initial complication.

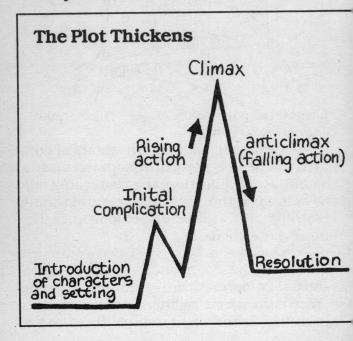

The Plot Thickens

Climax

Rising action

anticlimax (falling action)

Inital complication

Introduction of characters and setting

Resolution

In *Rumpelstiltskin*, the initial complication is when the king locks the miller's daughter in the room and says that if she doesn't spin the straw into gold, she must die.

The initial complication sets the pace for the story, and it gives the story a direction.

• **Rising Action**

The plot is composed of a series of complications, or incidents. Once the initial complication starts the ball rolling, the story will continue with one incident building on the last one. This is called rising action.

The rising action in *Rumpelstiltskin* includes the dwarf's helping the daughter to spin the straw into gold, the marriage of the daughter to the king, the birth of the baby that the daughter promised to

the dwarf, and the dwarf's demanding
the baby as payment.

Each incident or situation
in the story is a little more
exciting than the last.
The pace of the story
increases, and the
incidents get
closer together
This is where
the largest
part of your
story will
take place.

WHAT'S HAPPENING?

RISING ACTION

EVENT

EVENT

• **Climax**

When the series of incidents reaches a
crisis point, it is called the climax of the
book. The climax is the high point, or
most intense moment, of the story. Often
the significance of the earlier incidents is
made clear at this point. This crisis is
often the basis for the growth or change
that all main characters undergo.

The climax of *Rumplestiltskin* is when
the queen's messenger overhears
Rumpelstiltskin dancing around the fire,
singing the song about his name. Now
you know the queen will guess the dwarf's

name and save her baby. The danger is passed.

• Anticlimax

The action in the story begins to slow down following the climax. This period of falling action is the anticlimax. The crisis has not been cleared up yet, but the stress of the situation seems to lessen.

The anticlimax of this story is when the queen finally guesses the name, and Rumpelstiltskin tears himself apart in rage.

• Resolution

Fortunately, there is hope for your main characters in the form of a resolution. The resolution of a story is its outcome. At this point the plot brings together the loose ends of the story and solves the problems presented in the book.

Of course, not all problems are solvable. If a main character has died, the author really can't bring him back to life! The resolution of a book isn't necessarily a happy ending. It should be a realistic solution to the problems encountered in the book. As in most fairy tales, the resolution of *Rumpelstiltskin* is—you guessed it—that they all live happily ever after!

How to Use Your Literary Lingo

All of this information about the language of book reports will help you when you gather the facts for your work sheet. The work sheets in the following section are designed to help you do all your research before you begin writing.

There are three work sheets. Each one is for a different type of book.

1 Fiction work sheet

You can use the fiction work sheet with any type of fiction book, including romance, science fiction, fantasy, and mystery books. Fill out as much of the sheet as you can while you read. This will make writing your report easier in the end.

Fiction Story Work Sheet

Due date: _____

Title: _____

Author: _____

Publisher: _____

Date/place published:_____

Book type (mystery, science fiction, etc.): _____

Setting

Time period (era/season): _____

Place: _____

Characters

Main characters (Describe each one, and tell how they change in the story.):

Protagonist: _____

_____

_____

_____

Antagonist: _____

_____

_____

_____

Other main characters: _____

_____

_____

_____

Minor characters: _____

_____

_____

_____

_____

Plot

(Summarize the action in the story.):

_____

_____

_____

_____
_____
_____
_____
_____

Mood
(What were some of the moods in different scenes in the book?):_____

_____
_____
_____

What was the author's purpose in writing this book? _____

_____
_____

Opinion
(Did you like or dislike the book? Would you recommend it to a friend? Tell why):

_____
_____
_____
_____
_____

2 **Autobiography/Biography work sheet**
The questions on a work sheet for autobiographies and biographies are

phrased a little differently from the fiction work sheet. The books are similar in many ways, but there is an important difference. The story, the setting, and the characters in a nonfiction book are real.

Autobiography/Biography Work Sheet

Due date: _____

Title: _____

Author: _____

Type (autobiography/biography): _____

Publisher: _____

Date/place published: _____

Subject's name: _____

Place of birth: _____

Family members: _____

The subject is best known for: _____

Give three major events in the subject's life: _____

_____

_____

_____

_____

How did the subject react to these events? _____

_____

_____

_____

_____

_____

Would you recommend this book? _____

_____

_____

_____

3 Nonfiction work sheet

Other types of nonfiction books such as how-to books, history books, self-help books, or reference books have a separate work sheet. These books are written to teach you something. They do not have characters, settings, or significant incidents. This work sheet is based on what you learned and how you benefited from reading your nonfiction book.

Nonfiction Work Sheet

Due date: _____

Title: _____

Author: _____

Publisher: _____

Place/date published:_____

Type (how-to, reference, history, self-help): _____

What was the main purpose of this book? _____

_____

_____

_____

_____

Why did you want to read this
book? _____

_____

_____

How can you use the information from
this book? _____

_____

Would you recommend this book? _____

_____

_____

Once you've completed a work sheet for
your book report, you're ready to write.
Don't be nervous. This is a "You Can Do
It" guide, and you *can* do it! In the next
chapter you'll learn how to use these
work sheets to pull together a great book
report.

4 *Putting it all Together*

You did the hardest part when you gathered all the details about your book and completed the work sheets in Chapter 3. Now it's time to put it all together in the final form.

Tie Up the Loose Ends

Before you get started writing, make sure you've done the following things.

• Finish your book!

This is your last warning. Your teacher knows when you are patching together a book report. Read the whole book! Don't attempt to summarzie a book based on the blurb that's on the back of the book jacket. Don't try to write a whole report after reading only half of the book.

• Read book reviews.

One way to get an idea of how to write a book report is to read a few book reviews in a magazine or newspaper. Book reviews condense the story into a few paragraphs, and then they give an opinion of the book. Notice how the reviewer summarizes the action. Also pay attention to how she expresses her opinion.

- **Follow your teacher's guidelines.**

Your teacher has specific guidelines that you should follow when you write your book report. Make sure that you understand how your report should look before you get too far into the writing process.

Teacher's Guidelines
Before you write your report, ask the following questions.
• When is it due?
• Should it be typed or handwritten?
• How wide should the margins be?
• How long should it be?
• Should it be double-spaced?

The work sheets included in this book will be helpful in gathering information. But they're not a substitute for any guidelines or forms that your teacher gives you.

Begin at the Beginning

Okay, it's time to get down to business! Gather your work sheets and your book. Get a pen and some paper. Find a quiet, well lighted place.

Now, start writing.

If you need a little help getting started, begin your book report with the following information.

THE BEGINNING

• **Identification of work**

Your report should begin with the title and author of your book. You don't have to start out with "The name of my book is *blah-blah-blah.*" Try something a little different, like "An interesting experience got John Doorknob started on writing *The Story of a Nerd* in 1986." This way you give the important material in a different way.

- **Type of book**

You're writing a book report, not a murder mystery. So don't leave your teacher in suspense! Your next step is to define the type of book you read. Don't just say that it is fiction. Try to use a clear label such as science fiction, romance, or humor. This information should be on your work sheet already, so you won't have to think long!

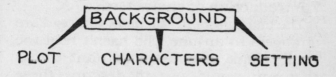

- **Background of the story**

Your next step is to give a little bit of background information for your book. Tell about the plot, the characters, and the setting. You are still introducing your book, so don't give too many details yet.

This section should reveal just a taste of your book. A touch of suspense makes your report more enjoyable. If you were writing a report on a book about a girl whose new puppy causes all sorts of disasters in her life, you could say, "In the spring of 1988, Jennifer Smith got a puppy for her 13th birthday. That is when her troubles began."

Don't start your report with "The book I read was about—" This kind of opening has been known to put teachers to sleep. Try to be a little different. Think about your book and its plot. Find the initial incident that starts the action in your book. Use this situation as the background for your opening paragraph.

• Introduction of characters

The characters in the book you read are strangers to anyone who hasn't read the book. Think of a few important things that you would use to describe these people if you were introducing them to your best friend. Don't get too detailed, but don't leave out anything important. Try to create a mental picture of the character.

• Introduction of setting

The setting of some stories is just as important as their characters. If this is true for the book you read, then make

SETTING

sure that you give
plenty of detail about
the time and place
the story took place.

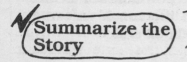

Summarize the Story

The heart of your
book report is the
summary of the
action. Don't try to
tell everything that happened. Some of
the incidents are just not as important as
others. If they did not move your story to
its climax or its resolution, then don't
include them here.

Choose at least three events that were
important to the outcome of your book.
Tell what happened, and tell how your
characters reacted to the events.

All of these incidents should lead up to
the book's climax and resolution. Describe the climax of the book, unless it
spoils too much of the story for someone.
Make sure that you don't give away too
much of the ending, though. Your book
report should inspire other people to read
the book. Do you think they'll want to
read it if you've spoiled all the surprises?

Report-Writing Rule

Tease them, but do not tell them! Don't spoil the surprise for your friends. They may want to read the book sometime, so don't give them too much information about how the book ended.

✓ Finishing Touches

The first version of your book report should now have information about the story, the characters, and the setting.

Quotations ""

ADD

PIZZAZZ

What's missing is the extra finishing touches to make your book report great.

Here are several ways to make your book report stand out.

• Use quotations.

Quotations tell a lot about a story. You can use a direct quotation (a quote which uses exact words) from a character. Direct quotes help the reader to picture the character. Authors try to make each character talk differently. The character's choice of words tells a lot about his personality.

You could also use descriptive quotations to add some flash to your report. A descriptive quotation is one that tells about the action, the characters, or the setting without using dialogue. You could use this type of quotation to introduce your setting, for example. Using a descriptive quotation also helps to define the mood of the story. Think about Snoopy's favorite opening line, "It was a dark and stormy night."

• Make a comparison.

If you've read other books by this author, you could use your knowledge of her other stories to make a comparison.

Try to find the common idea in the two books, and weave this into your report.

A comparison doesn't have to be long and complicated. Your comparison could be just one sentence, like "Both *The Story of a Couch Potato* and *The Story of a Lamp Post* by John Doe are comedies about fifth-grade boys who can't seem to do anything right."

- **Tell the author's meaning.**

Some books have messages or morals. A moral is the knowledge about life and about right and wrong that the author wants to pass along to you. Not every story has a moral. But if yours does, then make sure that you include it in your report. The message can be really important, like "People shouldn't use drugs." Or, it can be less important, like "Lima beans aren't really that bad if you just give them a chance."

End at the Ending

The final part to your report should be your opinion of the book. Be honest.

If you didn't like the book at all, then say so. If you loved everything about it, say that, too. If you thought it was sort of good but had some boring parts, then include that in your report.

Whenever you give an opinion about a book, support it with evidence from the book. Your teacher wants to know why you said what you did. Your reasons will also help your classmates decide whether or not they want to read the book.

FINAL PART: YOUR OPINION OF BOOK

The End

Polishing Your Paper

Before you turn in your book report, check it over very carefully for any errors in grammar and spelling. Are your classmates and teacher going to have any respect for your opinions about the book if they notice that you misspell the word *the?* Maybe they will, and maybe they won't. But why take the chance? Proofread carefully.

Make sure that you have followed your teacher's guidelines. Read the report out loud to hear how it sounds. If your sentences are choppy or confusing, correct them before your teacher does.

Rewrite your book report, and make all the corrections needed. If you are writing it by hand, use your best penmanship. Make sure that your margins and the length of the report are what your teacher has requested.

Now, turn in your report!

Oral Reports

At times your teacher may assign an oral book report. Don't be tempted to just

read your written report out loud. Oral reports are a special form of presentation. They deserve a little extra care to make them interesting.

There are four important things to remember when you are giving an oral report.

1 Posture

When you are standing in front of your class, stand up straight. If you

are a little nervous, then hold on to the edges of the podium. This will help improve your posture and make you look more confident. Don't slouch or shuffle your feet. Stand still, and look at your audience. Take several deep breaths, and go for it!

2 Practice

You wouldn't try a double flip off the diving board without practicing first. Don't give your oral book report without a little practice either. Even if you get nervous before you give an oral report, you'll feel more confident with a little practice. Try giving your report in front of the mirror a few times. Look straight at the mirror while you talk. You might feel a little silly, but it pays off! Keep your head up instead of looking down at your notes. With enough practice, you won't need to look at your notes very often.

After you've practiced alone for awhile, find a live audience. Your parents are probably good guinea pigs. Even your baby sister will do, if necessary. Practice as many times as necessary until you feel confident that you can give your report smoothly.

3 Patterns of speech

Have you ever really listened to yourself talk? You may be in for a surprise. Most people use certain expressions over and over again without realizing it. Others say "uh," "I mean," or "you know" when they get nervous. You may have your own expression that you use without thinking about it.

The only way to *really* hear yourself is to tape-record your oral report. Set up a tape recorder during one of your practice sessions, and then play back your report when you're finished. Are there certain words that you overuse? Do you speak too quickly or too slowly? Now practice again, and try to correct these problems.

4 Props

An oral presentation goes over well if you have something to show to your classmates. Of course, the handiest prop is the book you are reporting on. Other props could include a poster, a map showing where the story took place, or a costume that could have been worn by a character in the book. Use your imagination to think about what would work with the book you have read.

5 Projects with Pizzazz

Not all book reports follow a specific format. Sometimes your teacher may allow you to do special book report projects. And that's great news for you! Why? Because book projects let you use your creativity and imagination to communicate the same information contained in a written book report. We're talking fun here! Let your imagination take off. But before you get too crazy, make sure of a couple of things first.

Check It Out!

As in any project you do for school, you should make sure that your project is acceptable to your teacher before you start working on it. Summarize the plan for your project in a paragraph, and give it to your teacher well in advance of your due date.

Once your teacher has approved your book project, you still need to make sure that you follow all the rules. Does your teacher have guidelines you need to follow? Does it need to be a written project? Or, can it be some sort of artistic creation? Do you need to work with another student on a dramatic presentation? Find out early, and follow the rules.

Book projects can be divided roughly into written, artistic, or dramatic presentations. The next few pages contain lots of ideas for projects in these three categories. You'll be able to think of lots more. Maybe these ideas will spark more ideas for your own creative projects.

The examples use fairy tales. You're familiar with the characters and the action of the stories. This background information will make it easier to apply the knowledge to your own book project. But remember not to try to do a project on one of these fairy tales. They're only examples.

Written Book Projects

1 Advice column letter

This project would work well for both serious and funny books. Write a letter to an advice columnist, like Ann Landers or Dear Abby, and pretend that you are the main character in the book. Explain a little bit about your situation, and then ask for advice.

Imagine an exasperated young girl asking for advice on her special problem.

Dear Abby,

I am a young princess who used to live in a beautiful castle. Now I live in a tiny little cottage in the woods with seven dwarfs.

I have two big problems. First, my wicked stepmother is always trying to have me killed because she is jealous of my good looks. I don't mean to brag, but I really am the fairest one of all. Why can't she just accept me as I am?

My second problem has to do with a bad habit of the seven dwarfs. They whistle. They whistle while they play. They whistle while they eat. They whistle while they work. It's enough to drive a young girl crazy!

It's not enough that I am in constant danger of being rubbed out by my stepmother, but should I also have to put up with this gross whistling? All day they whistle, whistle, whistle while I clean and scrub the house. I ask you, should the fairest one of all be providing maid service for a bunch of ungrateful, whistling slobs?

Signed—Not too fond of apples

P.S. Will my prince ever come?

As silly as it is, you've still told a lot about your main character and her situation. You know that Snow White is beautiful, and that her stepmother hates her and wants to kill her. She keeps house for seven dwarfs who whistle a lot. She is waiting for her prince to come. You've even planted a hint that apples play a part in the fairy tale.

2 Newspaper story

Another good way to reveal story and character information is to write an article as it would appear in a newspaper. Newspaper articles have a lot of information in the first paragraph. The next few paragraphs give details about the information in the first paragraph. A newspaper article should give the factual information without opinions.

Here's a late-breaking story from the *New Pork Times*.

SATURDAY MARCH 18 . . . .

NEW PORK TIMES

WOLF BURGLAR FINDS HIMSELF IN HOT WATER

An unidentified wolf was admitted to County Hospital Saturday evening following a freak chimney accident. Witnesses said the wolf had attempted to break down the door of a brick house before climbing onto the roof and jumping down the chimney.

The owner of the home, Mr. L. Pig, had a kettle of scalding water in the fireplace at the time. The wolf suffered second and third degree burns over the lower portion of his body.

Mr. Pig told police that the wolf had attempted earlier break-ins at the homes of his two younger brothers. The younger Pig brothers had filed charges on Saturday afternoon after the wolf attempted to huff and puff and blow their houses down. The two houses were made of hay and sticks. Neither of the younger Pig brothers were worried about the possible damage caused by the wolf. They were reported to have said, "Hey diddle, diddle" and played on their fiddles.

"Who's afraid of the big, bad wolf?" asked the Pig brothers. The wolf had no comment. He was being held on a charge of breaking and entering.

This type of book project allows you to tell as much about a specific incident as you wish. You wouldn't want to try to cram all the book's action into the article. Choose a scene that is important to the story or that tells a lot about the characters.

3 Epilogue

An epilogue is the story of what happened after the story ended. Books aren't like movies, which always seem to have a series of follow-up movies called sequels. Can you imagine *Goldilocks and the Three Bears: Part II*?

Use your imagination and your sense of humor to decide what might have happened after the story ended.

Goldilocks has taken a job at the Feels Just Right Mattress Company as a mattress tester. She gives mattresses a grade of "too hard," "too soft," or "just right."

Mama Bear has started selling her homemade soup. Her motto is "It's not too hot, and not too cold. It tastes just right." She and Papa Bear have made enough money to

replace the chair that Goldilocks broke, and they've saved some money for Baby Bear's college fund.

The epilogue is a great place to tie up the loose ends of a story. You get to decide what happens. You could get revenge for something bad that happened to your favorite character. You could patch up a broken romance or get even with a bully. Don't get too crazy with this approach. Make the events believable, and base them on things that really happened in the story.

4 Movie script

A movie script contains information on the setting, the character, and the action as well as the dialogue.

Lights, camera, action!

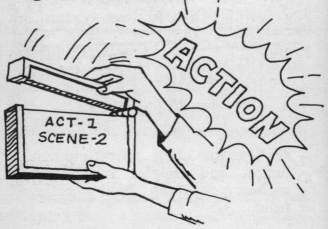

Act 1, Scene 2: The Ball Invitation Arrives

(Setting: The hearth of a stately home in the Kingdom. Cinderella is seated on the stones trying to get warm. She is covered with cinders and ashes.)

(Enter stage left, the stepsister Drucilla carrying a white envelope)

Drucilla:	*(speaks with excitement)* An invitation to the prince's ball!
Prunella:	Oh, what will I wear?
Cinderella:	Yes, what will I wear?
Drucilla:	**(laughs with scorn)** What will *you* wear, Cinderella? Why, you'll wear what you always wear to clean out the cinders!
Prunella:	Surely you don't think you can go to the prince's ball, Cinderella! You're just a maid and an orphan. You don't belong at a prince's ball.

(The stepsisters leave, stage right. Cinderella is left alone at the hearth. She holds the invitation in her hand.)

Cinderella:	Oh, I wish I could go to the ball. I wish I could have a beautiful gown and dance with the prince. If only I had a fairy godmother!

Use the dialogue to help convey whether the characters are happy, sad, mean, or snobby. Describe the setting and the characters so that somebody playing

the part could act, move, and dress
properly.

 Interview

Magazines often have interviews with
famous people. How about a question and
answer interview with one of the characters in your book? You could also make it
a talk show script, like this.

See if you can guess who this mystery
guest is.

Question: Please welcome my special
guest. **(loud applause and
cheers)** I like that green suit.
Is it true you live in a large
oak tree with a lot of other
fellows?

Answer: Yes, that's true. But it's
really a very nice tree.

Question: We've heard that you have
a strange habit. Can you
tell us a little bit about
that.

Answer: You're probably referring
to my habit of stealing
from the rich and giving
to the poor. I really don't
think of it as a *strange*
habit. It just seems fair to
me.

Question: How do the authorities feel about your sense of fairness?

Answer: The Nottingham sheriff isn't too fond of my activities. His guards are always chasing me and my merry men around Sherwood Forest. His niece, Maid Marian, thinks I'm pretty nice, though.

Question: Is there any truth to the rumors that you and Maid Marian will be getting married soon?

Answer: I really don't think I should comment on that.

KID'S MAGAZINE

Special INTERVIEW WITH MYSTERY GUEST

You are correct if you guessed that it's the world's most famous archer, Robin Hood. You can use this format to reveal much about the story and setting by asking the right questions.

6 Book review

Book reviews in magazines or newspapers briefly give details about the setting and characters. Their emphasis is on the reviewer's opinion of how well the book is written.

In a traditional written book report, you give your opinion of a book, but it's mostly information about the story. A book review is a little different because it emphasizes your opinion. Book reviews don't give as many details about the story because a reviewer doesn't want to spoil the story for the readers.

Does this review make you anxious to read the book?

Sleeping Beauty is about the Princess Aurora, a young princess who was cursed by an evil fairy when she was born. The curse is that when she pricks her finger on the spindle of a spinning wheel she will sleep forever. A good fairy changed the curse so that she would wake up with a kiss from her true love. When she turns 16 years old the curse takes effect, and she falls into a deep sleep.

Frankly, this story seems a little weird. The author doesn't make the characters seem very real. We hardly get to know the Prince, and Princess Aurora seems too good to be true. Okay, she's beautiful. And he's handsome. But what are they really like? We just don't know from this story.

The two main characters don't even get together until the last part of the book, and the author expects us to believe that it is true love. What a fairy tale! How could two total strangers live happily ever after? This type of story just encourages the wrong idea of marriage. Doesn't the author know how high the divorce rate is?

BOOK REVIEW
by ME, ACE REVIEWER

SLEEPING BEAUTY
STINKS!

7 Letter to author

Have you ever enjoyed a book so much that you wanted to write a fan letter to the author? Why not do it, and turn it into a book project? This is your chance to ask the author anything at all about the book.

If you decide to mail your letter to the author, use the address of the publishing company on the title page of the book. Publishers will forward mail to their authors.

8 Dinner party

Make a guest list for a dinner party for your characters. Choose food that is appropriate to the story. Write out invitations, and plan the decorations. You could even make a seating chart, which is a plan that shows where people will sit at the dinner table. Make sure you don't seat the villain next to the hero, or a mouse next to a cat!

9 Poem

Poems don't have to rhyme, and they don't have to be long. Free verse is a type of poetry that doesn't rhyme or follow a certain pattern of rhythm. Limericks or jingles are short, usually just four to six lines, but they are packed with information.

Your poem should contain information about a character, a part of the story, or even the setting. It doesn't have to be about the most important characters or actions, though. For example, a poem about Little Red Riding Hood wouldn't have to be about the wolf or about Red Riding Hood. It could be about how scary being alone in the forest can be, or how Red Riding Hood feels when she wears her red cape.

10 Prologue

A prologue is the part of the story that takes place before the opening scene of the story. It is the opposite of an epilogue. In the prologue to a book, you set up the story development and help explain some of the actions that will follow in the book.

A prologue to Snow White and the Seven Dwarfs would explain what happened to Snow White's mother, why her father married her wicked stepmother, what happened to her father, how the dwarfs came to live in the forest, and other things.

11 Character profile or feature

A character profile is an article written about a person which might appear in a newspaper or a magazine. The article makes the person interesting to us by telling lots of details. Not everybody in your book is colorful. Make sure you choose a character who is interesting enough to keep the reader's attention.

The story's action and setting are not as important in this type of project. You need to concentrate on an individual character, and write enough about her to let the readers get to know her.

12 Cast your story

Have you ever read a book and thought that you'd love to see it as a movie? Why not do a book project that involves choosing actors to play all the parts. Choosing the actors or actresses for specific charac-

CHARACTER PROFILE } INTERESTING

ters is called casting the story.

Find the perfect actor or actress to play the roles of the main and minor characters. If you can't think of someone famous to play the part, try casting your friends or other people from your school.

☆ MY BOOK ☆
STARRING
RIVER CLEVELAND
☆ AS ☆
THE BIG BAD WOLF!

Dramatic Book Projects

If you are a little bit of a ham, you could create a fun book project that you can act out. Most of the following ideas need more than one person. Check with your teacher first to see if this is okay.

1 Two-person movie review

A fun type of dramatic book project is a two-person movie review. A movie review is similar to the book review that we discussed earlier. Emphasize your opinion of how well the book was written, rather than describing the actual plot.

You and a friend should read the same book. For your presentation, place two chairs slightly facing each other. One person discusses his opinion first. The second one may agree or disagree. At the end of the review you can both grade the book with a number of stars, a thumbs-up, or a thumbs-down.

2 Game show

There are plenty of game shows that would make a good basis for a book project. If your book is a romance, you could base your dramatic presentation on *The Dating Game* or *The Newlywed Game.* If your book has lots of conflicts and fights, try something like *People's Court.*

Just make sure that your game show is appropriate to your story and to your characters. You play the part of the Master of Ceremonies. You may have to get several of your classmates involved in this project, so make sure they've read the book.

The game show project doesn't have to have every word planned, but don't make it too casual either. A little planning will keep you from getting tongue-tied and keep things from getting out of hand. As Master of Ceremonies you are in charge of making sure that things run smoothly. Have the appropriate questions prepared, and make sure your friends know what they have to do in the show.

WELCOME
TO
BOOK
OF
FORTUNE!

3 Debate

A debate is a discussion where two people take opposite sides. You and a friend should read the same book and decide on the topic of your debate. Topics of debates are generally expressed as questions. One example of a debate topic is "Should *Snow White* be required reading for sixth graders?" Another idea is to debate something that a character did in the book. For *Robin Hood*, try "Was the Sheriff of Nottingham justified in arresting Robin Hood?" or "Is it right to take from the rich to give to the poor?"

After you decide on the topic, pick sides. In debating, the side that favors something is called *pro*. The side that objects to something is called *con*. One team begins by presenting evidence to support its opinion of the topic, based on information from the book. After a set time period, the other side gets the same amount of time to present its side of the story. Then, each side gets a shorter rebuttal period to answer the opposite team's attacks and objections.

Your classmates can then vote on which side had the more convincing answer to the debate question. The side with the most votes wins the debate.

4 Dramatic reading

In a dramatic reading, you take a section of your book and read it out loud with lots of feeling. Descriptive sections with lots of dialogue make an interesting dramatic reading. If you read conversation from more than one character, make sure that you change your voice so that your listeners can tell the difference between one character and another. Ham it up, or play it serious. Pick a good scene, and really get into it.

You could also do this by having a friend read the part of a second character and a third person read the descriptive parts in between the dialogue.

5 Sales pitch or advertisement

A sales pitch is a dramatic presentation in which a character tries to sell something. Your character might have even tried to sell something in your book. To do this project well, you have to understand the character and pick some product that seems appropriate for him. The wicked stepmother in *Snow White* could try to sell poisoned apples. The Tin Man in *The Wizard of Oz* could sell metal polish or rust remover. And Tom Sawyer could sell—what else?—white paint. Use your imagination. This project can be as wild and crazy as you can make it!

6 Talk show

This is a dramatic version of the question and answer interview (number 5) we discussed in the written presentation section. All the people who take part in this presentation should read the same book. One person acts as host. The rest of the people could be characters from the book. The host interviews the characters one at a time or in a group. Make sure that you have your questions set up ahead of time. You don't have to write a script for the characters, but give them an idea of the questions you will be asking so that they won't be unprepared.

7 Puppet show

Here is a good way to use your dramatic skills without anyone ever seeing your face! You could make your puppets if you are artistic, or just use some from the toy box. Choose a scene with lots of characters and dialogue. The Master of Ceremonies can set up the scene and explain what's already happened in the story.

8 20 questions

This is an old game that works well with some book projects. Most of the people in your class should be familiar with the book and its characters. The book should have lots of characters to choose from so the game won't be too easy to solve.

Pretend that you are a character from the book. Your classmates have 20 chances to ask you questions. The questions must be able to be answered with either a *yes* or a *no*. For instance, your classmates can't ask how old you are, since that kind of question requires a longer answer than just *yes* or *no*.

9 Soap operas

If your book has lots of action and characters, it might be a suitable soap opera book project. Soap operas have lots of horrible things happening to their characters. The characters always react in dramatic ways.

Get a few of your friends to play the

parts of the characters for your soap opera. You will have to write out a script that shows all their dialogue and actions. Practice a few times before you have to give your presentation.

An important thing to remember is to overact! Nothing is unimportant in a soap opera. Even the smallest problem can cause deep depression, hysteria, or rage!

10 Mysterious moments

If you have read a mystery or a suspense novel, then you might consider putting together a small mystery party as your book project. Carefully choose a scene from the book that involves several characters and is crucial to the outcome

WHO DONE IT?

of the story. You'll need to write a script for each character. Make sure that you don't give away too much of the story in your scene. The idea is to leave your audience wondering "who done it?"

After you present the scene, take a vote from the audience to see if they have guessed the outcome.

✔ Artistic Book Projects

If you have a special talent for art, you might want to create an artistic book project. You know what you are capable of doing. Choose from this list, or make up your own project idea.

1 Map

Some stories are perfect for map making. If your story takes place in several locations, you could make a route map that shows where the action started and finished. Be sure to mark all of the landmarks that are important to the story. A book that has a journey in it is also perfect for this project.

Even if your story takes place in one small area, you could draw a map that shows the streets and houses where your characters live. Be sure to indicate things like their school and their best friend's house. Make certain that all the important places are on the map.

2 Portrait

Draw or paint a scene, an important event, a portrait of one of the characters, or anything else that you can think of from the book.

Don't just copy the picture off the book jacket or cover. Use your imagination. Find the information in the book that you need to make the picture. For example, the color of a character's hair and eyes, or the length and style of a character's hair can help you to draw or paint a portrait of the character.

3 Cartoon panel

Make a cartoon strip or even a comic book of your own based on the book. Cartoons with more than one panel are

called strips. Each panel contains a picture and balloons with dialogue.

Cartoons don't have to be funny, but your classmates might appreciate them more if they are. Find a scene or situation in your book, and draw a few panels about it. Include the dialogue to explain what is happening in the story.

4 Mural

A mural is a large art project that is usually painted on a wall. For your book project, you can paint your mural on a long roll of paper.

Murals don't have to be about a single scene in the book. You can draw all the characters in many different situations. Draw enough to let your viewers understand what the story is about.

Look in an art book to see some examples of murals if you need some help getting started.

5 Book jacket

The book jacket tells a lot about a book. The jacket's job is to make you want to pick up the book and read it. Have you ever chosen a book because you liked the jacket but then been disappointed in the story? In that case the jacket designer did a better job than the author!

A book jacket has several parts. The front cover has the name of the book and the author. It usually has some art work, although some covers just have words. The back of the jacket has what is known as a *blurb*, a short introduction to the story that is designed to make you want to read the book. It might also contain quotations from other people who have read it and liked it.

The front inside flap of the book jacket contains more detailed information about the story. The material continues on the back inside flap. The back flap usually has information about the author and sometimes a photograph of the author.

6 Poster

Making a poster about a book can be a fun art project. You can draw, paint, or even cut out pictures from a magazine to make a poster that shows an important scene, character, or setting.

You can also make a poster in combination with many of the other book projects presented in this section.

7 Collage

You have been doing collages ever since you started school. They are a fun and easy way to get across an idea.

Use old magazines to cut out pictures you think are right for your book. Collages look great if you include some headlines from magazines or newspapers, too.

8 Puzzle

This is a different approach for a book project. Draw or paint a picture that shows an important scene in your book, then cut it up like a jigsaw puzzle.

Make sure that you don't cut it out in straight lines. Make curvy pieces like the jigsaw puzzles you see in the stores. This makes it easier to put back together.

9 Diorama

A diorama is a three-dimensional project that is usually built into a shoe box. Draw and cut out objects to create the scene that you are representing. Glue them to cardboard so that they will stand up.

Now in one end of a shoe box cut a viewing hole that's big enough to see through. Tape the figures in position inside the box. Make sure that some of the items are up close and some items are farther back. Draw background scenery on the inside of the box.

Once you put the top on the box, the diorama will look like a three-dimensional scene from the book.

10 Mobile

A mobile is a set of objects attached by thread to dowels, thin sticks, or coat hangers. To create a mobile for your book project, try to think of some objects or symbols in the story. A mobile about *Jack and the Bean Stalk* might have a bean, a cow, a giant, and a bean stalk on it.

You can make these objects out of clay, draw pictures, or cut out pictures from magazines. It's neat to mix pictures and real objects, like a picture of a giant and an actual bean.

11 Sculpture

Making a sculpture of one of the characters or of an entire scene can be a good book project. If you make your sculpture from clay that needs to be fired, make sure that you leave enough time to get this done. Ask the art teacher at your school about using the kiln to fire your sculpture. Other materials you could use are papier mache, plaster of paris, wire, or any other materials that you can glue together, like sticks, wood, or other objects you find.

Attach your sculpture to a board with a label that gives the title of the book, the author, and the name of the character you have sculpted.

12 Advertisement

An advertisement is the artistic version of the commercial or sales pitch (number 5) explained in the dramatic book projects section.

Choose something that's appropriate for your character to sell. Design the page as it would appear in a magazine or newspaper. Be sure to inlcude some *copy,* or written information that describes the product.

✓ Where Do I Begin?

All the ideas in this book are just the beginning! You can use them for starters, and pretty soon you'll be thinking of lots of your own ideas. Remember, it takes a lot of imagination to write a book. So you should use your imagination also to come up with lots of great ideas for your book reports and book projects.

Remember to ask for your teacher's approval before starting on a special book project.

And don't forget to have fun!